Can authority bring freedom?

Rules book

Contents

Activity Symbols

Writing
Task

Thinking and
Reflection Task

Drama
Task

Partner or
Group Task

Art and
Craft Task

Reading
Task

Religious Symbols and Colours

Christianity ✝

Judaism ✡

Hinduism ॐ

Islam ☪

Special Words

When you see words in the text that are bold and underlined like **<u>this</u>**, there is an explanation of its meaning in the glossary on page 41.

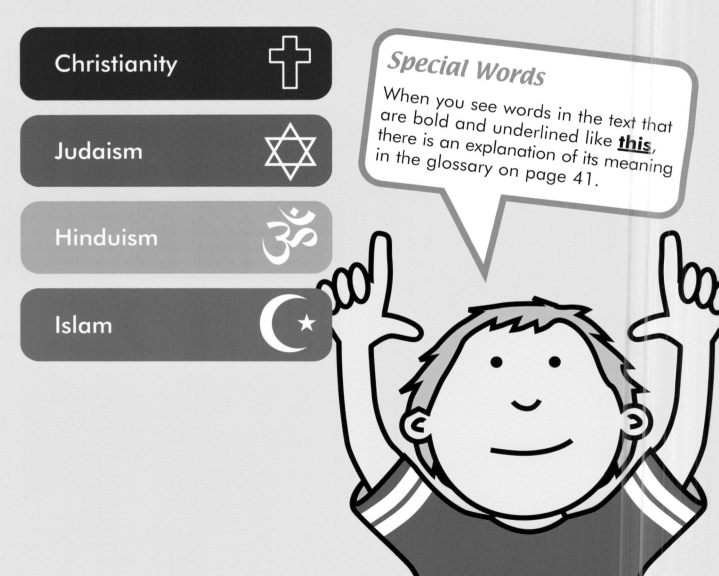

Can authority bring freedom?

This may sound like a strange question at first, but it is a question many people come to ask as they grow up. Everyone wants to be free, but there also have to be people in authority – and rules.

So sometimes it seems that authority and freedom are opposites.

So, what is 'authority'? And what is 'freedom'?

Are they total opposites of each other?

Can a person accept authority and yet be free?

Can anyone be completely free to do anything they wish?

Should all people in authority expect complete obedience?

Why do I have to listen to them...?

Why do I have to do my project when all my friends are playing football outside?...

I'm glad I listened to mum and dad!

PROJECT AWARD

Discuss as a group or a class the questions above, and see if you can come to some conclusions – even if you have to agree to differ from each other!

It would be a good idea to make a wall display of the different aspects of Authority and Freedom. You can add to it as your studies continue through this book. Perhaps start with the questions listed on page 1, and then add some of your different thoughts – using speech bubble or thought bubble shapes.

Check it out!

Before we go any further, let's just make sure we all agree about what we mean by 'authority' and 'freedom'.

If you look in a dictionary, you will find these kinds of definitions:

AUTHORITY

- legal power or right
- group or body of people in control
- personal influence through character, job, or moral qualities

FREEDOM

- being free
- no boundaries
- not influenced by anything

Have these definitions changed any of your thinking and discussion earlier? Talk about it now to a partner.

The interesting thing is that many religious people believe that there is a way in which being under authority can lead to a real sense of freedom – and we shall find out about that in the rest of this book!

Rules, rules

What is 'law'? What are 'rules'?

 Try looking in a dictionary to see what the words mean; make a note of their meanings. Take some time to look at them before reading on.

The meaning shows a law is really something that:

▶ gives direction

▶ shows the way people should live and behave

▶ is like a signpost which tells you the way to go.

Signposts are very useful for drivers and walkers.

In just the same way, laws and rules show people the way to live.

Not all rules are written down. You probably have quite a lot of rules in your family – things that everyone in your family knows.

 Talk about these as a class or with a partner. What sorts of things are these 'rules' about?

Note them down in a house-shape; your teacher may give you a worksheet for this task.

When we think about rules we often think they are negative things — because they are often written in a negative way:

- No Cycling!
- No Entry!
- Do Not Walk on the Grass!
- It is forbidden to . . .

Even your school rules may be stated in a negative way — like those shown opposite — but many schools try showing them as positives instead.

Take two of your school or class rules and turn them into positive rules. Then think of two or three more and write them negatively and positively.

DO NOT RUN!
WALK!

Information/cross curricular link:

You have probably done work in science or maths on positives and negatives, perhaps to do with a thermometer, or with numbers.

On temperature scales, **positive** (+) readings are those above **zero** (0); and **negative** (-) readings are those below it.

Your teacher may suggest you do some Literacy work on positives and negatives, such as black/white; good/evil; kind/selfish; etc.

SCHOOL RULES

Do not run in corridors.

Don't talk while others are speaking.

Do not talk during school assembly.

Don't take what belongs to others.

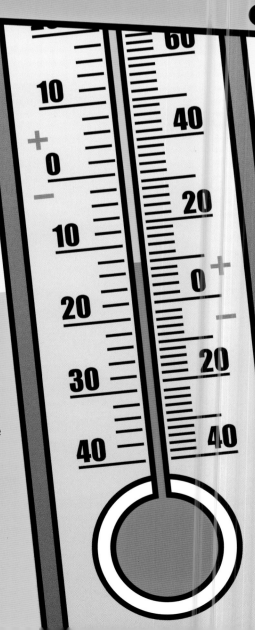

4

Worship no gods but me.

Do not worship idols or other images.

Do not use the name of God for evil purposes.

Remember the sabbath day and keep it holy.

Respect your father and your mother.

Do not commit murder.

Do not commit adultery.

Do not steal.

Do not accuse anyone falsely.

Do not wish for other people's things.

As well as rules in families and schools, there are rules in communities, and in religion too.

Probably some of the most well known are the Ten Commandments. Your teacher may tell you about them if you have not heard about them before.

Like many sets of rules, they appear negative – as it is much easier to say what should <u>not</u> be done, than to list all the things that <u>should</u> be done.

Choose five of the Ten Commandments and re-write them in a positive form.

Be glad for all that your neighbour has!

Rules try to help people follow the right things and keep the wrong things out of their lives. They are meant to be like a 'force field' – protecting and guiding.

Think about what rules try to 'keep out'. Draw your own version of a force field, with the 'aliens' labelled. Your teacher may give you a worksheet .

So, as rules are there for a reason, they must have some importance.

Sometimes we think it cannot be so serious, but think about it: if a rule has a purpose, then just taking no notice of it is likely to lead to a problem or difficulty.

Think about a football match – if players simply ignored all the rules, it would be impossible to play the game! If people driving cars and lorries took no notice of the rules, then there would be total chaos on the roads!

God rules

For many religious people, there are duties and laws that are part of their way of life as believers. These rules are very important, for they set out what is expected of them by the God whom they worship, or the community of faith to which they belong. And within many religions there is also a common understanding that rules and laws in society come from God – the One who has created all things.

So it is not surprising to find that most religions have a rule that is common to them all – what has become known as 'The Golden Rule'. It seems that every religion and society has the same principle.

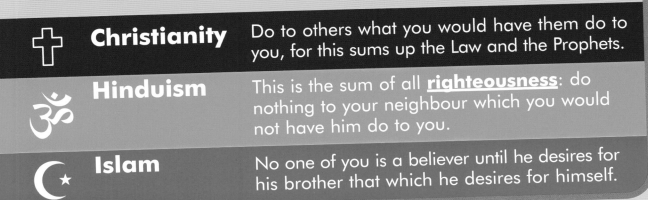

Golden Rule from Christianity, Islam and Hinduism

Christianity	Do to others what you would have them do to you, for this sums up the Law and the Prophets.
Hinduism	This is the sum of all **righteousness**: do nothing to your neighbour which you would not have him do to you.
Islam	No one of you is a believer until he desires for his brother that which he desires for himself.

What do YOU think of the Golden Rule? Write down your thoughts about it and give reasons for your answers. Then write down what you would like to do or to want for someone in your class.

(For example, you might want someone to be good at maths, because you know they find it difficult; or you might want someone in a wheelchair to be able to take part in more of sports day; or perhaps you might want to take someone from your class on holiday with you to Disneyland, as you know they have never been.)

A Christian Story

'Once upon a time there was a man – a man like any of us – who was travelling from Jerusalem to Jericho. Now as you all know, that is a very dangerous road. It's twisty and it's steep, and there's no end of places for robbers and thieves to hide.

Well, the robbers were waiting that day. And they grabbed the man. And they beat him. And they took his money and left him to die.

In a little while, another man came walking down that road – a priest, on his way home from worshipping God at the temple. He saw the dying man ..... but took one look at him and

continued on the next page...

A Muslim Story

Muhammad went every day to the mosque to pray. Near to the mosque lived a woman who did not like Muhammad, and who was often unkind to others.

Muhammad taught the people not to cheat, nor be unkind. He told them they should not worship **idols**, as so many of them did. A lot of people liked to do these things, so they were not happy to hear what Muhammad said.

The unkind woman who lived near the mosque liked to cheat, and be unkind, and she liked to worship the idols – it was what she had always done. So each day she waited for Muhammad to pass her house on his way to the mosque.

continued on the next page...

crossed to the other side of the road, and walked away.

"Oh my," the crowd murmured.

"Wait," Jesus continued. "Soon another man passed by. He served God at the temple, too. So what do you think this man did when he saw the wounded traveller?"

"He ran for help!" shouted someone.

"He raised the alarm!" shouted another.

"No!" said Jesus, again. "He did not. Just like the priest, he crossed to the other side of the road and left that poor man to die."

"Oh no," the crowd sighed.

"Don't worry," said Jesus. "For there was one more man who passed by that day. And he was a Samaritan."

"A Samaritan?" shouted someone. "They're different from us!"

"We hate Samaritans!" shouted another.

"And they hate us!" added a third.

"So I've heard," nodded Jesus. "But when this Samaritan saw the man, he did not walk away. He bandaged his wounds. He loaded him on his donkey. He took him to a nearby inn. And he paid for that man to stay there until he was well."

Jesus looked at the man who had asked him the question. "So tell me," he said, "which of these men was a neighbour to the man who had been robbed?"

"The third one. The Samaritan," the man answered.

"That's right," Jesus smiled. "Because my neighbour is anyone who needs my help. Now go and help your neighbour too."

When she saw him coming, she would sweep some rubbish together just outside her house. Then, as he passed her, she would sweep all the rubbish over him.

One day, the woman was not there when Muhammad passed by her house. He wondered where she was, as she was always waiting for him. He asked what had happened to her, and some women told him that she was in her house and was sick.

Muhammad went into the house. The woman was lying down, and crying. The house was very dirty. But Muhammad lit a fire, and cleaned the house. Then he prepared a meal for the woman.

When the woman saw how kind Muhammad was, she was sorry and ashamed for being so unkind. She became a Muslim, and promised to try to be kind to everybody.

- Discuss what similarities there are in the stories and list them. Then try to give a reason why these two religions have stories with such similarities.

- Complete a 'Comparison Alley' sheet, or a Venn diagram sheet of the two stories – your teacher may give you a worksheet for this. (Can you find out a story from another religious tradition that is also similar?)

What do Christians think?

God gives the rules

because He only wants the best for us

So Christians want to follow them

but they need help

because people do lots of wrong things

A 'new start' is needed

so...God sent His son Jesus

The Bible tells people about Jesus' life and teaching

which shows people how they should live

Jesus' death and resurrection gave people hope

because forgiveness comes and God's power lives within.

Many Christians believe that laws or rules themselves do not stop people wanting to do wrong things.
But asking God for help will enable people to work towards God's individual plans for their lives.

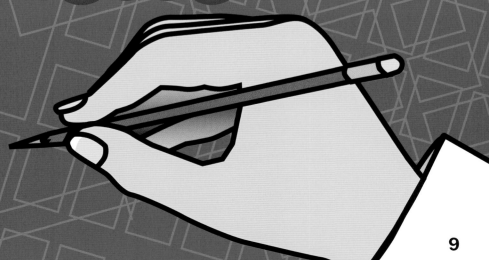

Good Teacher, what must I do to receive eternal life?

Read this play script about a man who kept the rules, but couldn't bring himself to really do what God wanted (it is a Bible story – you can find it in Luke 18: 18 - 30):

Narrator: As Jesus was starting on his way, a man ran up and knelt before him.

Rich man: Good Teacher, what must I do to receive eternal life?

Jesus: Why do you call me good? No one is good except God alone. You know the commandments: 'Do not commit murder; do not commit adultery; do not steal; do not accuse anyone falsely; do not cheat; respect your father and mother.'

Rich man: Teacher, ever since I was young, I have obeyed all these commandments.

Narrator: Jesus looked straight at the man with love and then he spoke warmly to him.

Jesus: You need only one thing. Go and sell all you have and give the money to the poor, and you will have riches in heaven; then come and follow me.

Narrator: When the man heard this, gloom spread over his face, and he went away sad, because he was very rich.

Think about the story, and make up a telephone conversation between the rich man and a member of his family or a friend.

Try acting it out (with either just one side of the conversation being heard, or both sides – whatever is your choice).

The Rich Young Ruler was a good man; he had to give up just one thing for Jesus, but he couldn't do it, as it meant too much to him. He loved his wealth and his lifestyle more than he wanted to follow Jesus' teaching.

 Think about the challenge Jesus gave to the rich man, and try to work out the issues the man had to decide on. Use a 'see-saw' or 'tri pie' diagram to record your answers. (Your teacher may give you a worksheet for this).

Then try to work out what really mattered to the rich man, and what really matters in life. Use two 'bull's eye' type diagrams with three circles:

centre circle – most important

next circle – quite important

outside circle – least important.

Here is a case study in our lifetime. Think about this person's response.

Richard Taylor is a Christian Minister.

But he has not always been a good citizen!

He lived in Wales when he was young, and when his parents split up he began to get into trouble at school - and out of school too! He did not feel loved or wanted, and lived for himself.

He began to play truant, and then to steal. He stole anything he could. He got into trouble with the police – but it didn't make him stop. He just went on stealing: he thought that money and possessions would make him happy.

Eventually he started to take drugs, and then he had to steal even more.

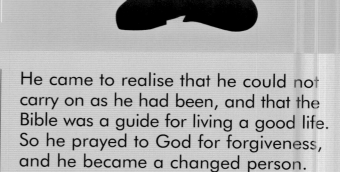

Finally he ended up in prison. There was no hope now – he had blown it!

He came to realise that he could not carry on as he had been, and that the Bible was a guide for living a good life. So he prayed to God for forgiveness, and he became a changed person.

When he came out of prison, he went to study to be a minister and is now in leader within a Christian Church.

Write a letter to Richard Taylor – what would you like to ask him about his experiences?

Or, if you prefer, just make a list of questions you would like to ask him.

Do a 'hot seating' activity based on the story, taking turns to be Richard, and try to answer questions in the way he would.

Draw a fortune line graph of Richard's life, showing his emotions at different times. (Your teacher may give you a worksheet for this.)

But one day he wanted something to roll cigarette tobacco in. He tore a page out of a Bible that was in his prison cell. He began to read it, and was surprised at what he read about Jesus.

The examples of the Rich Young Ruler and Richard Taylor show people having to choose - they had to open the door to follow God's way of life. This idea was painted by a famous Victorian painter called Holman Hunt. Study the picture – perhaps using a large edition.

What do you notice about the door? What does this tell you about what the artist meant by it?

What do you notice about Jesus? What does this tell you about what the artist was trying to say about Jesus?

Look up the Bible verse on which the painting is based (Revelation 3, verse 20). What does this add to your understanding of the painting?

[You might want to look up John 1 verses 4 – 5, and 9 verse 5 too].

I am the door

Jesus said, "I am the door"* – by which He meant that through His teachings and presence, people would find the right way to live their lives.

Think about the idea of a door and its uses. Try writing some sentences that show what Jesus meant.

Your teacher may give you a worksheet to help with this.

Knock! Knock!
Do you want to come in?
Knock! Knock!
Are you ready to change?
Knock! Knock!
Do you see a different you?
Knock! Knock!
Open up the door.

* Some versions of the Bible translate the saying in John 10: 7 and 9 as "I am the gate".

Choose the door

Some of the teachings of Jesus in the Gospel of Matthew are called 'The Sermon on the Mount', and are about many aspects of life. Let's look at just four main parts:

Getting your own back - or...?

"You have heard that it was said, 'An eye for an eye, and a tooth for a tooth.' But now I tell you: do not take **revenge** on someone who wrongs you. If anyone slaps you on the right cheek, let him slap you on the left cheek too. And if someone takes you to court to sue you for your shirt, let him have your coat as well.

And if one of the **occupation soldiers** forces you to carry his pack one kilometre, carry it two kilometres. When someone asks you for something, give it to him; when someone wants to borrow something, lend it to him."

Showing off - or working quietly?

"Make certain you do not perform your religious duties in public so that people will see what you do. If you 'show off' in public, you will not have any reward from your Father in heaven.

So when you give something to a needy person, do not make a big show of it as the **hypocrites** do in the temples and on the streets. They do it so that people will praise them. I assure you that they have already been paid in full.

But when you help a needy person, do it in such a way that even your closest friend will not know about it. Then it will be a private matter. And your Father, who sees what you do in private, will reward you."

I'm giving £500 to Christian Aid!

BANK
Date
PAY Christian Aid
Five hundred pounds
only

What kind of riches last?

"Do not store up riches for yourselves here on earth, where moths and rust destroy, and robbers break in and steal. Instead store up riches for yourselves in heaven, where moths and rust cannot destroy, and robbers cannot break in and steal. For your heart will always be where your riches are."

What foundation have you built on?

"So then, anyone who hears these words of mine and obeys them is like a wise man who built his house on rock. The rain poured down, the rivers overflowed, and the wind blew hard against that house. But it did not fall, because it was built on rock.

But everyone who hears these words of mine and does not obey them is like a foolish man who built his house on sand. The rain poured down, the rivers overflowed, the wind blew hard against that house, and it fell. And what a terrible fall it was!"

15

In each of these four aspects of Jesus' teaching, He was suggesting that people could be 'freed' from the usual kinds of reactions.

Getting your own back - or...?

Getting your own back seems like a good idea when someone upsets you, but in the end, does it really help? Often, the problem just gets worse and no one benefits. So why do it?

Showing off - or working quietly?

In the end money and possessions aren't everything – they cannot buy you some things. Winning the lottery may solve your money worries; but it brings a lot of new and even worse worries!

What kind of riches last?

The trouble is, when people show off, it is obvious to everyone, and spoils things. Wouldn't it be great if people did not give in to it?

What foundation have you built on?

In many ways, Jesus was trying to say, this is exactly what people do with their lives – they just live any way they like, not really thinking what matters or gives a solid base. So it is not surprising when it all falls apart. But it is possible to do it differently.

Divide into groups of 3 or 4, and look at just two of the four areas of the Sermon on the Mount. You should prepare a summary of what Jesus' teaching means for people living today. Try to make a catchphrase too.

When you have completed your work, your teacher will ask you to report back to the class (your reporting back will help others complete the next tasks, so try to be helpful!)

Most people would accept that:

GIVING is better than **GETTING** but how many knew it was part of Jesus' teaching?

A lot of people would also accept that being a *Show off* is not the right way to behave - and this too is part of Jesus' teaching.

Most of Jesus' Sermon on the Mount is about living life in the best possible way – about

being a builder
not a wrecker

So, Jesus meant that the solid foundation of His teaching would ensure that a 'building' (a person's life) was:

fit for life
and one of greater freedom and purpose.

Make a poster that shows how some things are good foundations for life, and some things are negative and may not be helpful.

(Your teacher may give you a worksheet to help you.)

The next morning, when the single brother went into his barns, he could not understand why he still had the same number of bags of corn as he had had the day before. He knew he had taken six bags to his brother in the night, but somehow he still had all the bags he originally had.

The married brother also could not understand: he had decided to give his brother six bags of corn, yet still he had exactly the same number of bags as when they divided the corn between themselves.

And from that day on, every harvest time, when the corn bags were divided up, each brother secretly took six bags of corn to the other. They never told each other, or ever talked about it, and they never managed to work out how they always ended up with the same number of bags as they started with.

- What do you think is the moral of the story?

- Can you explain why the brothers gave the bags to each other, and why they did it in secret?

- Make a list of the things that you can appreciate in your life.

- What things have you got which you could give to others?

- Act out the story, making sure the moral comes through clearly. (Why not try making a 21st century version? What could you use instead of bags of corn?)

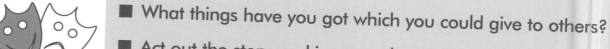

A Hindu Story

An old **Brahmin** priest lived in a holy place with seven disciples. In this holy place they worshipped and looked after some very old **deities** of Radha and Krishna. People came for many miles to see the Deities and make donations for their worship.

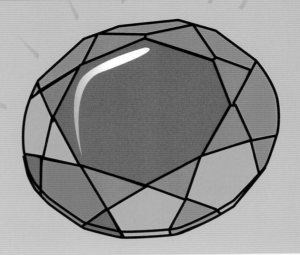

But the priest was growing old, and he knew he would soon leave his body, and he knew his disciples were not yet ready to be left in charge.

His fears were realised when one day a passing **pilgrim** donated a large ruby to the Deities.

"I think it should be sold and the money used," said one of the disciples.

"Not at all," cried another, "Radha should wear it."

A third disciple gave a different idea, "It would be much better to cut it into many small rubies, and make a beautiful necklace from them."

The disagreement lasted a long time, so much so that the Brahmin felt the Deities would never get the ruby. But he did not want to interfere, as his disciples had to learn to manage things themselves.

After a while, the Brahmin stopped the disciples from arguing, and told them to go off into the woods and bring back a stick no more than two and a half centimetres thick.

The seven disciples stopped their quarrelling and went off in obedience to their guru's command.

When they returned with their sticks, the old Brahmin took them and made them into a bundle. He tied them together with some rope. Then he asked them, "Which one of you can break this bundle of sticks?"

The seven young men took it in turns, but even the strongest of them could not do it. So they said to their **guru**, "It is not possible, master."

"Well watch carefully," said the priest. He cut the rope binding the sticks, and then took each separate stick and broke each one easily.

"I am getting old, and soon I will die. But you are like a bundle of sticks: if you try to help each other, work together and cooperate, then you will be strong, and will serve me well. But if you become divided and argue with each other, you will become weak and, like these sticks, will be broken. When that happens, who will care for our deities?"

The disciples understood the lesson and realised their mistake, and agreed to set the ruby into a ring, which could be placed on one of Krishna's fingers.

The priest was pleased that his disciples finally understood, and that he could leave them to manage the holy place. Soon after, he left his body and returned to the spiritual world.

When people came to see the famous deities, they often asked, "How did Krishna get such a beautiful ring?"

And every time the disciples answered: "By the strength of a bundle of sticks."

- What do you think is the moral of the story?

- Can you explain why the disciples could not agree?

- Make a list of the things that you often prefer to do yourself, or want your own way on.

- Collect a bundle of sticks and try it out for yourself.

- What things could you do just as well, or perhaps better, by working with others?

- Act out the story, making sure the moral comes through clearly. (Why not try making a 21st century version?)

- Now choose **one** of the two stories, and retell the stories in groups, using word cues.

Wise sayings

You have probably heard some wise sayings that have often been handed down from great grand-parents, and passed on from parents to children.

In groups of three or four, or as a whole class, share some of the wise sayings you have heard in your families.

When you have shared some of these, try to explain why they might have been passed on – what is it about them, or the things they are about, that might help explain it?

"Eat your carrots up - they'll help you see in the dark."

Maybe some of the wise sayings that you have discussed have not been all that important, perhaps not even very wise – but many people feel there are important teachings that are of great value for people of all ages and times.

Religious sacred writings contain sayings that people through history have come to realise are really wise. Something about the saying seems to have a 'ring of truth' – and yet, sometimes it is not as simple as that.

"Be careful who you choose as friends."

"Count the pennies and the pounds will look after themselves."

Read the three wise sayings below, and think about them carefully. They are from the book of Proverbs in the Bible, and will be read by Jews and Christians.

Idle working makes a man poor; hard work leads to a great fortune.

(Proverbs 12:27 - paraphrased)

Walk with the wise and your wisdom grows; but make friends with fools, and you will be ruined.

(Proverbs 13:20 - paraphrased)

Hate is always picking a quarrel; but love turns a blind eye to every fault.

(Proverbs 10:12 - paraphrased)

Say whether you agree, disagree, or are not sure about each proverb. Make a decision as a group, and explain to other groups the reason for your choice. Take a vote if the group is not in full agreement.

Now look carefully at the next three proverbs.

People who are bigheaded do not like to be corrected; they do not ask for help from wiser people.

(Proverbs 15 verse 12)

A smiling face makes you happy, and good news makes you feel better.

(Proverbs 15 verse 30)

People who are bad-tempered cause arguments, but people who are patient calm others down.

(Proverbs 15 verse 18)

Try writing one of the proverbs the opposite way around. For example:

"A miserable face makes you sad, and bad news makes you feel even worse."

Do you think it makes any difference? Why or why not? You could do this as a group task, and share your work afterwards.

Choose one of the proverbs to act out.

Make up one or two proverbs of your own. Write them out and act them out too.

Have you noticed how all these wise sayings are about building others up, and not wrecking things by being selfish or 'big-headed'? They share something with the teachings of Jesus we looked at earlier.

Here is a paraphrase from Psalm 19 of the Bible:

*The law of the Lord
is perfect;
It gives people strength.
You can trust God's
commands,
They make people wise.
God's laws are right,
They make people happy.
God's commands are fair,
They help people understand.
They are better than gold;
And sweeter than honey.*

■ Make phrases, using the starters below, adding your own ideas:

■ *They are more valuable than...*
■ *They are sweeter than...*
■ When you have decided, write them large enough for a display.
■ (You could use Word Art on the computer to create your sayings.)

The last phrase says that God's laws are better than gold or honey. In other words they are more valuable than one of the most valuable things, and sweeter than the sweetest known thing.

Why does the writer put it like this?

Because he is trying to say:

God's laws will last and last, forever

God's laws will always be there

God's laws will never end.

Here are some examples to get you started:

Sweeter than
▶ sticky toffee
▶ candy floss
▶ tea with three spoons of sugar

More valuable than
▶ a bank full of money
▶ the crown jewels
▶ my very best and favourite...

(You might also [or instead] like to do 'The Commands of the Lord' worksheet if your teacher has it.)

Wise words of Hinduism

Hinduism, like any religion, has ideas about right living.

One of the main ideas in Hindu teaching is to practice 'Ahimsa' – that is 'harmlessness'; something that would really make a difference to other people.

Ahimsa harmlessness

Another is to always seek the truth – in other words, to aim for the things that really matter, and that last.

Seek the truth

A good summary of doing this in everyday life is:

"Be clean, inside and out"

Think about these wise sayings in Hinduism, from the Bhagavad Gita, one of the holy books:

Sometimes you have to give up things to help people and to please God.

Never avoid doing your duty.

Be peaceful to everyone, even people you don't like and those who are unkind to you.

Choose one of the Hindu wise sayings. Now think of two different situations – one where it would be easy to follow the teaching and another where it would be hard. Describe each, and explain what you think a young Hindu would do and say.

Wise words in Islam

Most Muslims are careful to follow the teachings and guidance in the Qur'an, which is seen by Muslims as the words of Allah, and so has great authority.

Look at the saying to the right, and think about the sort of advice it gives to Muslims.

 Make up a simple picture-diagram in the form of a notice, to remind young Muslims of this important advice in the Qur'an. Design it as something to put on a wall or door as a reminder.

Worship none but Allah;
Treat your parents and relations with kindness, as well as orphans and those in need;
Be fair in your speaking to people;
Be persistent in praying; and practice charity regularly.

(Qur'an 40:83)

So? What's it all about - these 'wise' words?

Discuss as a class: "Everyone needs guidance to live the right way; it is part of being human."

Afterwards, note down the things that guide you in your life.

Obey God - not men!

This is a picture of Jesus that will probably surprise you.

Look at it carefully, and think about the questions below, and discuss them as a class.

▶ Is Jesus upset with someone? Who?

▶ Is He upset about something? What?

▶ Could He have been hurt or offended?

THE ANGRY *Christ*

Well, I hope you've been thinking:

"It must have been something very bad for Jesus to have been so cross!"

29

Well, here's what happened:

Place: Jerusalem, the capital city.

Building: The Temple (shhhh!... a very sacred place).

Occasion: Jesus visiting just before Passover time.

'I couldn't believe my eyes! There I was, sitting at my stall, minding my own business, when in came this chap. He looked troubled, and I said to my mate, "Aye aye! There's something big going to happen – watch out!"

'Well this man, he paced about a bit, and looked at all the comings and goings. It was a real market atmosphere, with loads of birds and animals, and money changing hands left right and centre. A bit chaotic really.'

'Well, then this fellow just seemed to make a move towards Benjamin's table and tipped it over – just like that! Everyone went scurrying here, there and everywhere. What a **kerfuffle**! People, animals and money scattering in all directions. Then suddenly everything stopped. Mouths dropped open and for a moment, no-one spoke. Then, as if that wasn't enough, he did it again, and again! Over and over went the tables. No-one knew what to do – it was **pandemonium**.'

Figs
Bananas

My house shall be...

'I shouted to my boy, Dan, "This is historic; this has never happened before in my lifetime."

And then this chap spoke over all the noise: "My house shall be a place of prayer, and you have made it into a den of robbers."

Everyone was asking who he was, and why he said it was his house. Then it dawned on us – it was Jesus! We had heard about him, and now here he was in Jerusalem. Well, he'd set a few sparks flying and heads wagging with this great performance in the temple. I wonder what will happen next?'

So what do you think?

Why do you think Jesus did it?

Should He have done it? Explain why.

Is there a time when you have seen something happen that made you angry? Talk about it to a partner; your teacher may ask for some stories to be shared with the rest of the class.

What makes you feel angry?

Many people would say that storing mountains of food (because the price isn't right) while so many in the world are starving, is something that should make us all angry.

Often we are told it is wrong to be angry. In many ways that is right – sometimes being angry is just us being selfish, or tired, or guilty. Most times, this sort of anger does not bring any goodness or any help to situations – in fact it just makes everything worse.

But anger that has a just cause, which is standing up for the rights and good of others, and which leads to something worthwhile and helpful, can be good.

Sometimes Christians talk of Jesus' anger in the temple as 'righteous anger', because:

▶ He was right to be angry

▶ what He did brought about change

▶ people began to think

- more about each other
- more about the community
- more about God and the temple.

1. Draw an equilateral triangle in the centre of a page, pointing downwards. Inside it, write: Righteous Anger

2. Draw a circle touching each side of the triangle.

3. In one circle, draw something you feel 'righteous anger' about from your own environment.

4. In another circle, draw something about world issues.

5. In the third circle, draw something from either area.

6. Use colours and symbols to show your strong feelings.

(Your teacher may give you a worksheet for this task.)

32

Do any of these make you angry?

- A bully knocking down an old lady
- An animal having a firework tied to its tail
- Making fun of someone who is not good at sport
- Discriminating because of skin colour or race
- Mocking a person who does not wear 'maker name' clothes
- **Jeering** at someone who struggles to do their work
- Destroying a Remembrance Garden
- Mountains of food held back
- Vandalising a children's playground

You might like to try a 'staircase parallelism' task here. (Your teacher may give you a worksheet for this.)

Staircase Parallels start with a simple statement (about what angers you), then the statement is extended (about things done to others that anger you), and then is extended again (about things in the world at large that anger you). For example:

There are many examples of people in the world who have spoken out against things that have angered them, or seemed very wrong and unjust.

Sometimes they were inspired by religious beliefs, and were prepared to suffer because of their actions; they felt that doing nothing was going against their beliefs. It was as if they felt they had to obey God, even if that meant going against a ruler or another human authority.

I hate being bullied.

I hate victimising those who are not the same as me.

I hate the injustices in the developing countries of the world.

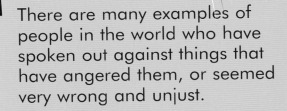

Speaking out

The classic Bible example is the story of Daniel in the Lion's Den. You can find the story in Daniel – Chapter 6 in the Bible. Read it, perhaps in a story version of the Bible, and try to complete one section on a chart like the one below.

(*Save the rest of the spaces till later!*)

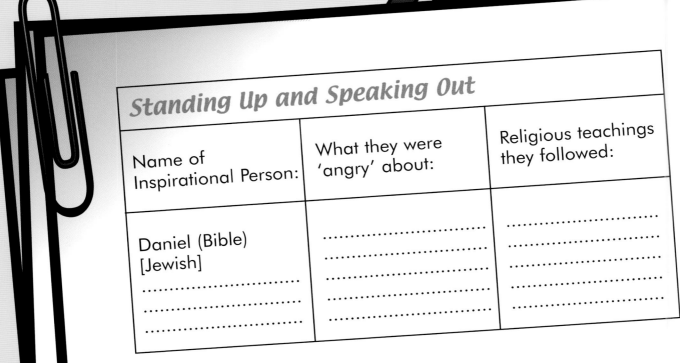

Standing Up and Speaking Out

Name of Inspirational Person:	What they were 'angry' about:	Religious teachings they followed:
Daniel (Bible) [Jewish]	....	....

On the pages that follow, there is a gallery of 'Inspirational People'. There is a small amount of information about each one.

Look through them, and choose **three or four** that interest you. You could find out a little more about them from books or the Internet, and complete the chart that you have started.

Think carefully about these people – their beliefs, their motives, their actions, the reactions of others (especially those in authority).

(Your teacher may give you a worksheet for this task.)

Maria Gomez

- primary school teacher in El Salvador
- active member of the Baptist Church
- regularly met with other Christians to challenge injustice and work for the good of the poorest people
- shot and killed in 1989; a special cross was **commissioned** to celebrate her life and faith

James Mawdsley

- Christian human rights protester
- made a stand for the rights of the Karen people in Burma
- imprisoned for five months for giving out leaflets and **campaigning**
- returned again to defend the rights of the people, and was given a 17 year sentence
- finally released, but still convinced people must stand up for justice

Rosa Parks

- **seamstress** from Montgomery, Alabama, USA
- refused to give up her seat on a bus to a white person, on 1st December 1955
- famous bus **boycott** began, leading to the Civil Rights Movement
- one of many Christian black people who believed racism was wrong and unjustified

Julia Neurberger

- one of the first women rabbis in Britain
- stands out against **discrimination** towards women
- involved herself in medical research issues, and became a member of the Interim Licensing Authority
- helped to set up the Inter Faith Hospice in North London
- **passionate** to cut through tradition and get morally right actions and decisions

Rabbi Hugo Gryn

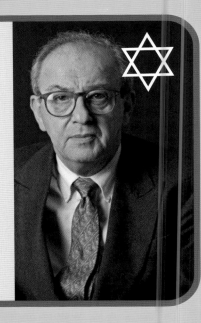

- sent to concentration camp by Hitler at age 13
- survived the experience, and trained in America to be a Rabbi
- marched with Martin Luther King in the Civil Rights Movement
- worked with refugees in India
- became Rabbi of West London Synagogue in 1964
- frequent radio broadcaster and public speaker
- always stood up against injustice and discrimination, and worked for peace and tolerance

Yusuf Islam

- famous pop singer, Cat Stevens
- converted to Islam in 1977 following a personal experience
- gave up his singing career to become a teacher of Islam
- founded a Muslim school in London
- passionate about peace and justice in the world

Rowshon Malik

- devout Muslim, living in Birmingham
- teaching and learning manager for English as a second language
- works for Birmingham City Council
- Director of the Bangladesh Women's Association
- a life long learner who believes education can solve many social problems
- campaigns tirelessly for the rights of all Asian women

Swami Vivekananda

- born Nanrendranath Datta
- became a religious hermit and devotee of Ramakrishna
- took part in the Parliament of Religions in 1893
- promoted the Ramakrishna Movement in the USA and UK
- a reformer within Hinduism promoting social and educational programmes
- worked to end child marriages, and to spread education

Akhandadhi Das

- born in Belfast, to a family of Christian Protestants
- became interested in Indian religious thinking and became involved with the Krishna Consciousness movement
- studied architecture at university, but went to live at Bhaktivedanta Manor in Watford, home of the International Society for Krishna Consciousness
- became president of the temple, and teaches others to look for spiritual satisfaction rather than worldly possessions
- stands up against discrimination and division between people of faith, and for the common truths of all religions

Free From and Free To

a) Choosing to be

We all have to make choices in our lives; and we can choose to be part of something bigger, or decide that we cannot make a difference! Sometimes it is simply seeing oneself in a different way; for example not just as a small weak thing (such as a petal) but as a part of something bigger and more impressive (such as a beautiful flower that is admired).

Look at the pictures below, and see if you can make phrases that show the choice we do have if we wish to take it. Here's an example:

We can help you, if you will let us.

I am only a wave, make me a sea.

b) Choosing to obey

When we obey the rules and laws, which are there for living life fully and enjoying it, we are choosing to become part of -

a pattern and purpose

that weaves us into

a beautiful and

exciting life experience

as we influence others
and are influenced by them -
in true freedom.

So, can authority bring freedom?

Through this book, you have discovered some very important things about answering that question:

The meanings of 'authority' and 'freedom', and of 'laws' and 'rules' • Rules are signposts for life • There is a Golden Rule common to most religions • Religions teach about new beginnings and hope • Standing up for injustice might mean breaking some rules • People have to choose their lifestyle • Anger about injustice and unfairness is not always wrong • Most rules are really positive but written negatively!

So when you think about it carefully, you'll see that we can choose to obey the highest religious rules/authority . . .

And when we do, we discover just how free we really are, and how much better life is for us and all around us!

Glossary

boycott	p.35	when people stop buying something or using something by way of protest
brahmin	p.21	Hindu name for a priest
campaigning	p.35	working hard to bring about something, or to get things changed
commissioned	p.35	when a person is asked and paid to do a particular task
deities	p.21	Hindu name for gods
discrimination	p.36	when people are treated differently because of their skin colour, language or gender, etc.
guru	p.22	Hindu word for a special teacher
hypocrites	p.14	people who pretend one thing but do or say another
idols	p.7	statues or models of gods
jeering	p.33	making fun of another person or group through sounds and actions
kerfuffle	p.30	people being noisy and making a fuss about something
occupation soldiers	p.14	soldiers who are in control of a country that is not their own
pandemonium	p.30	noise, confusion and everything in a mess
passionate	p.36	believing strongly about something
pilgrim	p.21	a person making a special religious journey (pilgrimage) to a holy or sacred place
revenge	p.14	getting your own back on someone
righteousness	p.7	being pure and always doing what is right
seamstress	p.35	a woman who sews and makes clothes as a job